Mel Bay Presents

# Christmas Eve

## 16 Solos for Celtic Harp

## By Sunita Staneslow

## WWW.MELBAY.COM

*Visit us on the Web at www.melbay.com — E-mail us at email@melbay.com*

# Contents

Sunita's **Christmas Eve** recording was her fourth album and is a unique collection of Scandinavian and German carols, arranged for harp in a reflective and improvisational style. Sunita's contemporary interpretations of this holiday music capture the spirit of Minnesota, a state that celebrates the Scandinavian heritage of much of its population.

Sunita has been playing music since she was a child. She studied with teachers in her native Minnesota and has travelled to learn from some of the great harpists of our time in New York, Paris and Tel Aviv. She graduated from Tufts University in Medford, Massachusetts and earned a Masters Degree from the Manhattan School of Music. Sunita has performed as principal harpist with the Jerusalem Symphony and the Minnesota Opera. She is a founding member of the ensemble Vida and the Celtic band Northern Gael.

After completing graduate school, Sunita's Scottish husband bought her a clarsach (Scottish folk harp). Together they travelled around the world for one year, harp in tow. Inspired by this experience, Sunita began performing folk music from a variety of traditions. She enjoys performing both on her larger pedal harp and her Scottish clarsach and uses both instruments for the different styles of music that she performs, often bringing them both on stage together. Sunita's work has been recognized by the American Harp Society, The Scottish Clarsach (harp) Society and the International Society for Folk Harpers and Craftsmen. She has released 12 recordings on the Maxemilian and Excelsior labels and is featured on two Windham Hill compilations in addition to appearing as a guest on numerous other recordings.

# Joy to the World

George F. Handel
Arr. by Sunita Staneslow

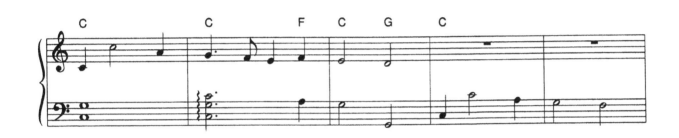

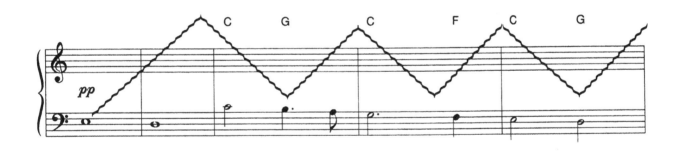

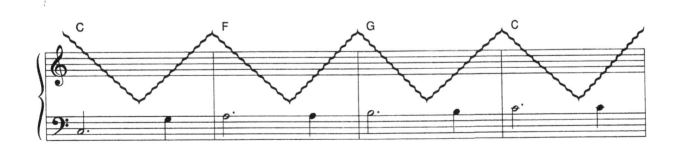

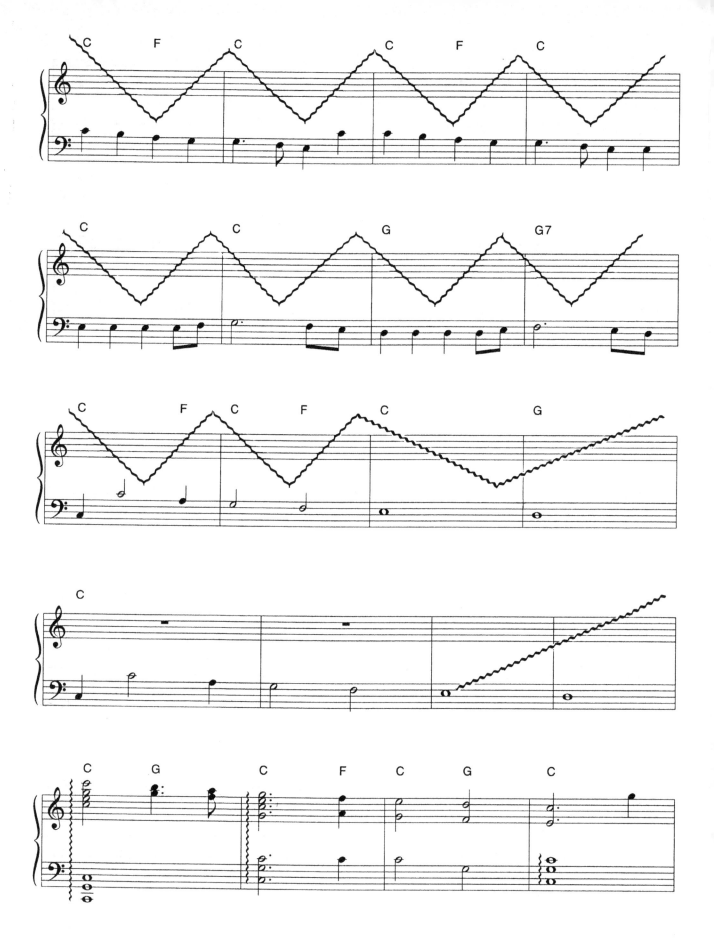

# From Heaven Above to Earth I Come

melody attributed to
**Martin Luther**
Arr. by Sunita Staneslow

9

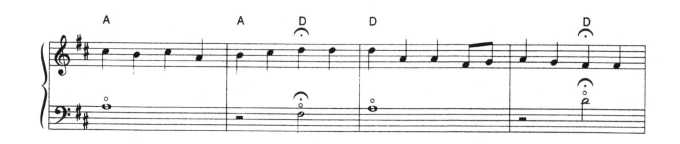

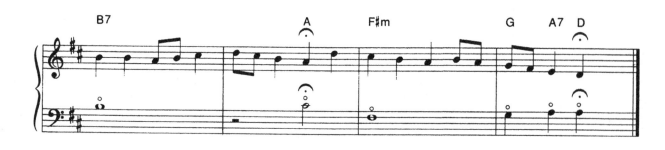

# When Christmas Morn Is Dawning

German folk melody
Arr. by Sunita Staneslow

# In the Bleak Midwinter

Gustav Holst
Arr. by Sunita Staneslow

16

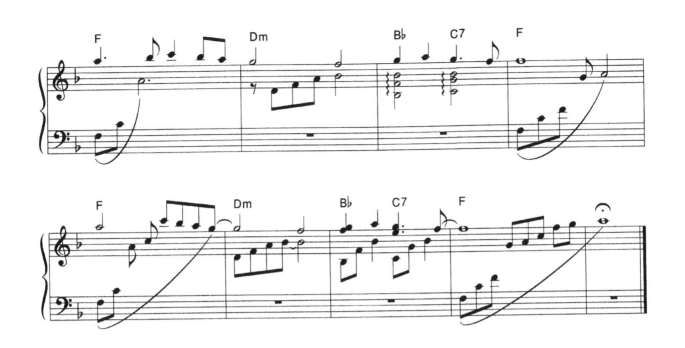

# A Child is Born in Bethlehem

Traditional Danish Carol
Arr. by Sunita Staneslow

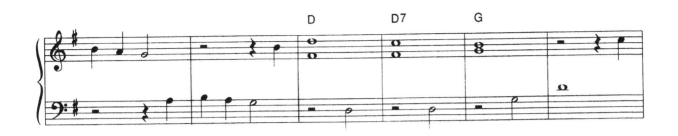

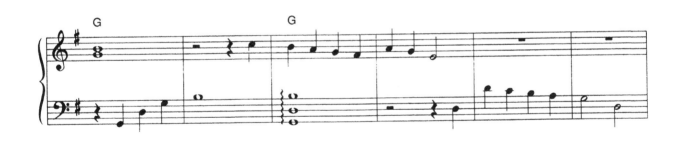

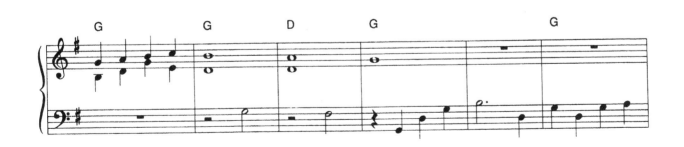

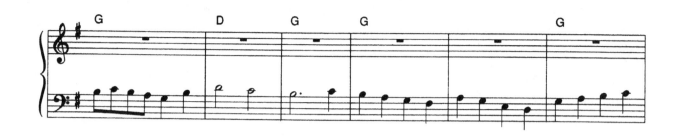

# Silent Night

Franz Grüber
Arr. by Sunita Staneslow

22

❀ Quickly and lightly roll chord
continuously throughout measure.

23

# Rejoice, All Ye Believers

Swedish folk song
Arr. by Sunita Staneslow

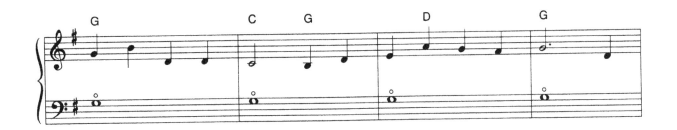

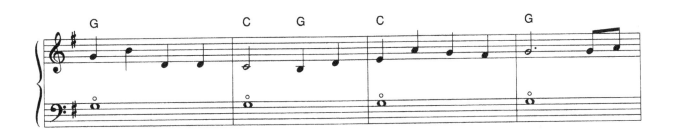

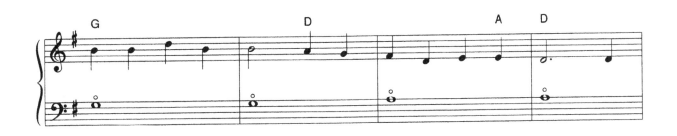

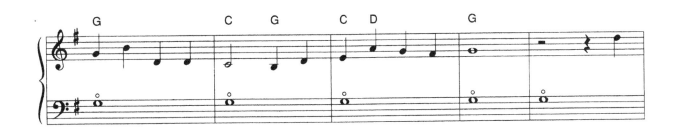

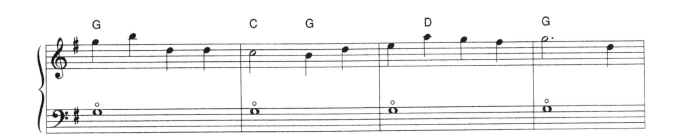

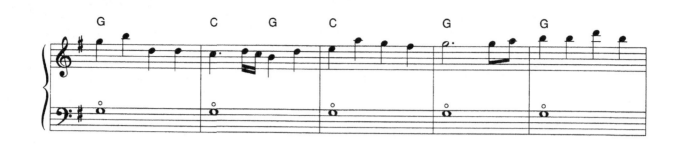

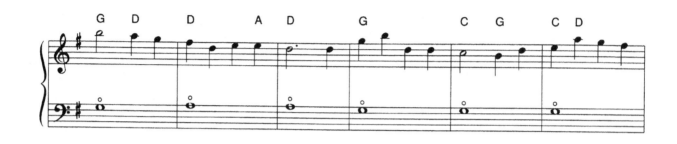

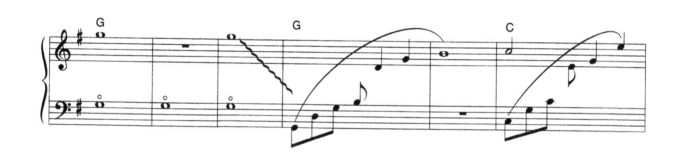

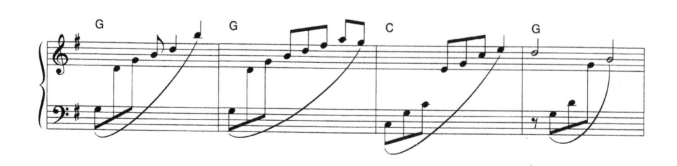

# I am So Glad on Christmas Eve

Peter Knudsen
Arr. by Sunita Staneslow

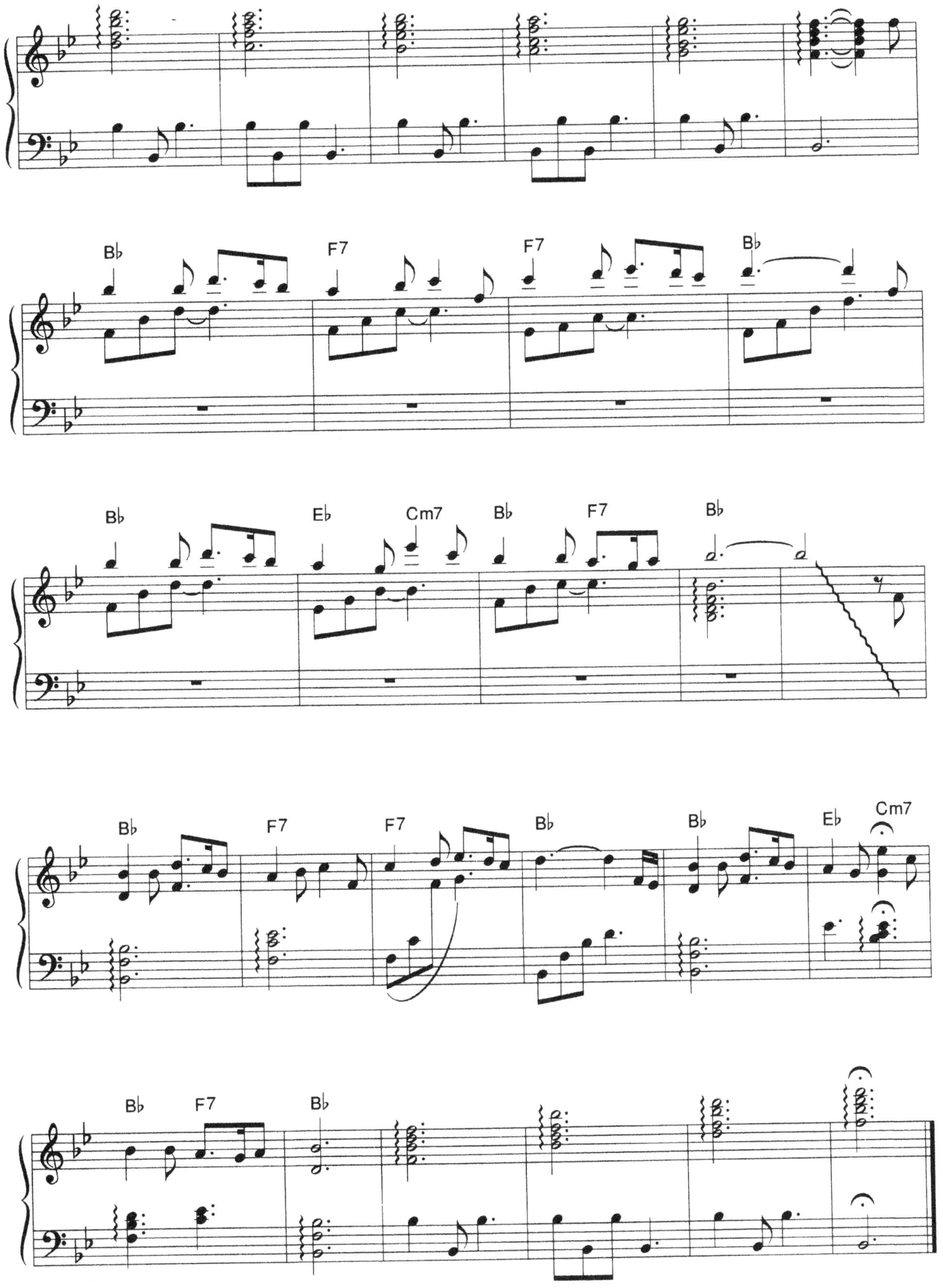
B♭
F7
F7
B♭
B♭
E♭
Cm7
B♭
F7
B♭
B♭
F7
F7
B♭
B♭
E♭
Cm7
B♭
F7
B♭

# Good Christian Men, Rejoice

Traditional German Carol<br/>Arr. by Sunita Staneslow

34

# Lovely Is the Dark Blue Sky

Trad. Danish melody
Arr. by Sunita Staneslow

# Lo, How a Rose E'er Blooming

Traditional German
Arr. by Sunita Staneslow

# The Happy Christmas Comes Once More

C. Balle
Arr. by Sunita Staneslow

43

# O Christmas Tree

Traditional German carol
Arr. by Sunita Staneslow

# Joseph Dearest, Joseph Mine

14th Century German melody
Arr. by Sunita Staneslow

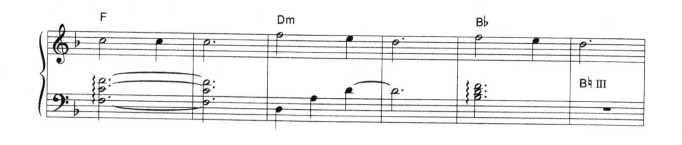

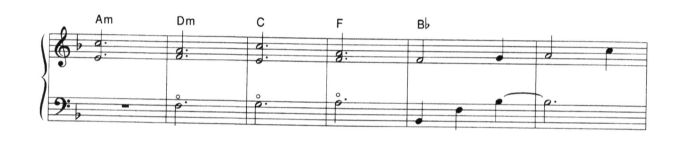

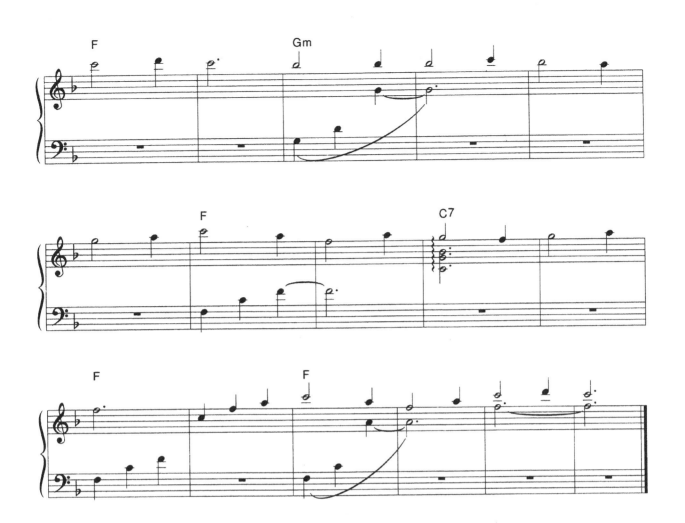

# While By My Sheep

Traditional German carol
Arr. by Sunita Staneslow

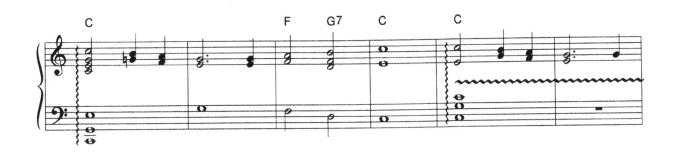

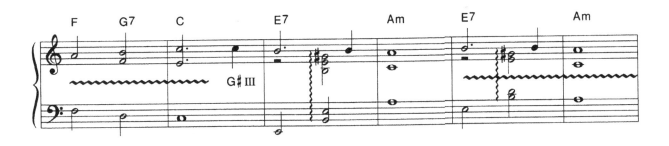

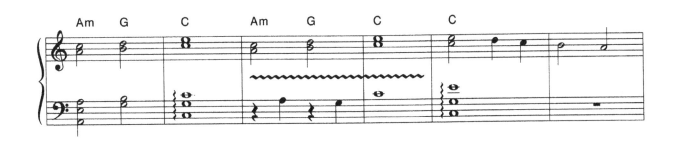

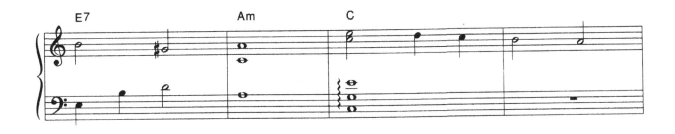

# O How Joyfully

from the Latin Hymn
"O Sanctissima"
Arr. by Sunita Staneslow

## Mist Covered Mountains
Sunita • *Celtic Harp*

*fiddle • Scottish smallpipes • flute • guitar • bodhrán*

Featuring some of the most popular Celtic tunes from Ireland and Scotland. The lilting sound of Sunita's harp, with some fine instrumentalists, gently interprets these traditional melodies. Includes: *Women of Ireland, Star of the County Down, Danny Boy, Morrison's Jig, Skye Boat Song, Plaxty Drew.*          CD only     # 20022

## Crossing The Shannon
Sunita & Northern Gael • *Celtic harp • fiddles •*

*smallpipes • concertina • flutes • guitar • bodhrán*

Crossing the Shannon takes the listener on a musical tour of the irish landscape, and celebrates the rich heritage of Erin's Isle. With rousing jigs and reels, songs and soulful airs, Sunita and Northern Gael share their love of Celtic tradition. *Includes: Crooked Road to Dublin, Roscommon Reel, Heather on the Moor, The North Clare Jig.*
CD only   # 20042

## Sunita Solo Harp   *Celtic harp*
Music from the Mediterranean Rim and the British Isles are woven together in a celebration of the instrument and its origins. The vibrant live sound was achieved through direct to digital recording in the Winton Great Hall of Minneapolis on an authentic Celtic harp made for Sunita in Scotland. Includes: *Scarborough Fair, Carolan's Draught, Eleanor Plunket, La Rosa Enflorece, Adio Querida, Adon Olam.*
CD # 20312   cass. #20314
Companion Book available from *Mel Bay*

## Acoustic Passion
Sunita & Vida • *harps • cello • percussion*

Acoustic passion envelopes the listener with romantic melodies and exotic rhythms combining classical music with ethnic and jazz traditions. From fiery interpretations of Spanish and North African melodies to jazz and gypsy rhythms, VIDA captures the essence of the era with a cross-cultural musical feast. Includes: *Villa-Lobos Aria from Bachianas Brasileiras No.5, Granados Spanish Dance No5, Brubek Blue Rondo á La Turk.*          CD #20512   cass. #21514

## Romantic Harp   Sunita • *harp*
*violin • cello • flute • French horn*

A collection of Sunita's favorite classical music performed with some of America's finest chamber musicians. These solo harp performances, duets, and trios are perfect for quiet dinners or curling up with a favorite book. Includes: *Ravel Pavane, Debussy Claire de lune, Bach Siciliano, Pachelbel Canon inD, Schubert Serenade.*          CD only #20032

## Romantic Harp II   Sunita • *harp*
*violin • cello • flute*

This collection of music by French composers captures the essence of elegance and sets the mood for quiet evenings, candlelight dinners and reflective meditation. Includes: *Fauré Aprés un reve, Satie Gnossienne, Debussy Romance, Saint-Saëns The Swan from Carnival of Animals.*
CD only #20072

## Boughs of Holly   Sunita • *harp*
*violin • cello • recorders • harpsichord • percussion • French horn*

Boughs of Holly includes many favorite English carols and a few lesser known gems. This combination of harp solos and ensemble performances is lively and full of Christmas magic. *Ding! Dong! Merrily on High, The First Nowell, We Wish You a Merry Christmas.*          CD only  # 20042

## Christmas Eve   Sunita • *solo harp*
Timeless carols from Sweden, Norway, Denmark and Germany. Sunita's contemporary interpretations of traditional festive music is perfect for creating the holiday mood. Includes: *Silent Night, Joy to the World, When Christmas Morn is Dawning.*          CD #20412, cass.#20414
Companion Book available from *Mel Bay*

## City of Gold   Sunita • *harp*
*violin • cello • oboe • English horn • clarinet • percussion*

City of Gold was commissioned and recorded in honor of Jerusalem's 3,000th anniversary. The grandeur of that legendary city is captured with Sunita's harp improvisations and orchestrations that are both meditative and inspirational. The recording was crafted with a full rich sound and appeals to a broad audience. City of Gold is a collection of passionate music written about Jerusalem through the ages and includes: *Jerusalem, On the Rivers of Babylon, Jerusalem of Gold, The Theme from Shindler's List.*   CD # 20612, cass. #20614

Traditional music for Jewish Weddings and other occasions. Includes four processionals and two recessionals. *Erev Shel Shoshaneem, Dodi Li, Erev Ba, Siman Tov.*

12 pages     book #10010

More wedding music including selections arranged in a more contemporary style than Volume I. *L'Kha Dodi, Artza Alinu, Bashana Haba'ah, Hevenu Shalom Alekhem, , Od Yishoma.*

16 pages  book #10030

This variety of Jewish melodies can be used for almost any occasion. The tunes range from Israeli songs to traditional folk tunes and prayers. Includes: *Adon Olam, Frailach, La Rosa Enflorece.*

12 pages  book #10020

Most of the music from Sunita's recording, City of Gold can be found here. Includes: *In Jerusalem, On the Rivers of Babylon, Jerusalem of Gold.*

22 pages   book #10050

Maximilian Productions, PO Box 40475, St. Paul, MN 55104, USA • Tel: 612-227-6041 • Fax: 612-227-0320 • Order line: 800-985-8040
Email: sunita@musicmax.com • Web: http://www.musicmax.com

16689520R00033

Made in the USA
Middletown, DE
24 November 2018